Table of

Chapter 1 – Life Forc
Chi, Spirit, and all that Jazz 3
Chapter 2 - Karma
All dogs go to heaven 10
Chapter 3 - The Path
Move it or lose it 20
Chapter 4 – Homemade Soup
Learning how to take our daily medicine 27
Chapter 5 – Quantum Physical
Understanding the inner workings of all bodies 36
Chapter 6 – Systematic Breakdown
The impact of negative energy 48
Chapter 7 – Laws
Know when you are about to be pulled over 55
Chapter 8 – Alchemy
Tools to survive going forward 65
Chapter 9 – Ascended Living
Grow, Live, and Love 71
Chapter 10 - The Calamity
Staying out of the pressure cooker 77
Chapter 11 – Trouble in Paradise
How when and why of coming Earth Changes 84
Chapter 12 – Library of Congress
Obelisk, Obel-that Keys to the Hall of Secrets 92
Chapter 13 - Suspended Animation
Time=Patience 100

To my family , my loving wife Mary Ann and my two beautiful children Hailey Olitha and Cody Tyee, for all their support and encouragement to begin this monumental undertaking of helping Mother Earth and all her family to heal, and regain their respect and natural balance.

Copyright © 2011
By
Konahwhaka

1chapter

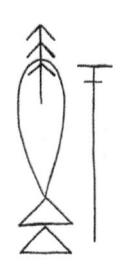

LIFE FORCE

Chi, Spirit, and all that Jazz

In the beginning, and in the beginning there was the first droplet of life force eked out of the Creator, the All in All, sparked into life which over great periods of time transformed eventually into all of the planets, the stars, man, and every living thing we could ever conceive it.

A master once explained it to me as the first tree of all of eternity was created and blossomed into the original first tree of life. As time continued in the natural cycle of nature or life, it began to drop its apples. Some decayed while others cracked open exposing the seeds of its life force still beating and seeking re-growth. As the winds rose they embraced the seedlings and gathering them in an effort to sow into the surrounding fertile earth, spreading them in a random but purposeful fashion. Many seeds flourished and more trees began to grow. Each new tree a completely different separate being and yet still all emanating from that very first glorious tree of life.

With many trees being completely different, some were more prosperous than the rest while even growing right next to each other. Different size leaves, branches, and even fruit, creating an image of vast differences yet alarming similarity. Each completely unique in formation to each other and yet still all brought into creation from that very first apple, falling from that very first tree, now so many years ago.

Were it not for the life force of the first tree in its living glory, shedding its newly formed life force of its fruit, none of the other trees could be witnessed this new day in their separate unique image, but all identical in that to the original life force.

That one drop of life force created an entire living orchard of new life. The cycle of which continues and evolves, even taking on different forms. As some apples rot and mold, not transforming into other trees, fungus is created along with other microorganisms. All creating and completing new cycles of life that again transform over time to other forms of life that eventually create a seemingly entire new planet of living, breathing things. Each still emanating from that first life-force, of that first fallen apple, of that first tree of life.

That is the master's simplified illustration of how we are all uniquely and seemingly separate beings that are inwardly created and exist only because of the original single drop of life force the Creator once sparked and released into the universe.

We are the same life-force, coming from the same original tree of life. Even though that first tree can no longer be found in the original orchard we are all the same. That is why we can talk to the trees, feel the ocean, and read the sky. We are all one. Anything else you try to believe is denying our true origins and true makeup.

Your soul is your life force and energy is your Chi. There are four separate elements that comprise the entire body that is living here on Mother Earth. The soul is the originating life force that is ignited by your individual flame that produces energy that animates or puppeteers the physical body.

A soul comes into a body of a child at 90 days of fetal development. Prior to that the mother is the sole supporter of both bodies by her own individual life force. With it the new infant brings with them the flame of life and it is placed just behind the navel, suspended between the soul (life force), the ethereal body and the physical body.

Each day the life force of an individual is ignited through the flame to create new energy in the ethereal body which animates the physical. We can receive additional new energy from outside forces, mainly through our chakra system, but we can only replenish our life force used each day by ingesting other forms of life force. Mainly food, be it plants or animals. We are literally transforming the other life force into ours in order to replenish it and keep the physical body animated and supporting the bodily elements.

That is why raw food is the most potent in the exchange of this life force continuum. Not enough new life force re-introduced into the body and we will, as anyone knows about self-survival, abandon the physical body and return to the outer dimensions where life force is not extinguished on a daily basis. There is no set qualifier of either plants or animals being right or wrong for us. Both can equally give us the refurbishment of our daily life force that is needed. It is the amount of life force present in the meal (or offering) and the intention in which it was raised, lived, sacrificed, and prepared, that equates to the amount of positive life force gained.

If it is raw and say just recently sacrificed, it will probably contain the greatest amount of life force available. Therefore the need for quantity is lessened. If it has been mechanically harvested, freeze-dried, frozen, corrupted (in various electronic manners), microwaved, or just plain bad old food, it has almost no redeeming life force and large amounts would needed to be consumed in order to satisfy our daily replenishment necessary to stay healthy and in the body. The body can extract some elements from the lower-grade food needed to help in the cellular regeneration of itself but nothing towards the replenishment of the soul.

Music is the tonic for the soul. Music is created and experienced on the 4th dimension. We presently exist on the 3rd so music has an instant elevating quality to it. Not only does it sooth the savage beast as they say, but it actually has the ability to heal on a soul level in a most profound and everlasting way. In shamanism the drums are utilized to entice the soul to change their vibration and to help it realize what some would characterize as instant healing. In its proper form it entices the negative energy to exit both the energy body and any blocked deposits surrounding the soul. That's why native music from many cultures has survived for so long.

Of course music can also have a seriously destructive quotient to it. Most heavy metal music while captivating, and to some even inspiring, typically is a destroyer of the natural etheric balance and thus can actually do damage to the soul with enough volume and continued repetition. Some in this modern society object to the language that usually accompanies it but it is a pebble in its negative impact compared to the damage the beat and frequency can inflict on the vibrational and energy fields of the body.

Modern warfare has now created many a dangerous and even life threatening instrument/machines of frequency and vibration in their quest to take warfare to the next level. Low frequencies can be used to illicit everything from sexual ecstasy to bodily malfunctions.

So as soul music is just that, an incredible flow of interwoven celestial sounds delicately played to elevate our consciousness, be very aware of music and its influence on your life force and body. May it be positive or negative, be as careful to what you listen to, as you should be as protective of what you eat. Both have direct access to the soul. And that gate should be heavily protected.

2 chapter

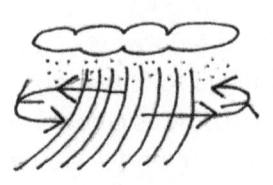

KARMA

All dogs go to heaven

Karma is the most commonly used spiritual term today in modern society and yet it is the least understood. There are relatively two types of karma that exist, soul karma and earthly karma. Each of these can be created and exchanged in three different ways; in the totality of all of your lives, in the progression from one lifetime to another, and in your daily learning and living of each and every lifetime. Both earthly and soul karma can have the opportunity to be intertwined and compounded in these expressions for greater effect and learning.

For instance if you were to choose to return to earth to learn the great spiritual lesson of humility, you would then create earthly and soul karma situations that enable you to create that learning for each. If you were a tyrant in a previous lifetime for no spiritual positive good or lessons, you may then return in your next incarnation to circumstances that teach you your errors in judgment, with spiritual and earthly karma mixed and working and teaching together. You make and redeem spiritual and earthly karma as you live out each specific lifetime and evolve in your daily experiences in each.

Depending on your successes with your growth in each lifetime, in terms of your soul or spiritual evolution, you can gain and release your soul karmic debt as you move along into new lifetimes. You carry soul lessons or spiritual karmic debt into each new lifetime along with sometimes a little unresolved earth karma. Karma gained can be both positive and negative from past spiritual and earthly sets of actions and deeds.

Earth karma is mostly created and paid off, as one may say, in our day to day living. For instance you were driving down the road and someone happens to cut you off in your car, never happens I know, you instantly react intellectualizing that they didn't have to do that and you squint your eyes and have a negative thought about them. Swear at them; hope they run out of gas, whatever. Presto, you have just created a negative earthly karmic debt or attachment for both you and the person you threw negative energy at. They now have to be cut off or incur a small injustice to pay off the debt you have just attached to them, really your intended purpose. BUT YOU must now yourself pay off a new karmic debt because you just created, with throwing negative attachments to this unknown driver, a karmic debt for yourself. It could have been avoided easily but you had to cast negativity by creating a negative judgment against another; an earthly karmic debt.

    Depending on how much karma you have piled up on your stack of debt will be a determining factor in how quickly you get the opportunity to release it. I wrote my first book 25 years ago and it was a book of sayings. To this day the one saying that never has left my consciousness is:

> The amount of time it takes for a persons'
> thoughts to manifest into reality
> is directly related to the distance they
> are from their true selves.

That has multiple applications but it is very potent in its application to both earthly and soul karma.

So when you cast that negative debt out with being cut off on the road. Depending on your debt backlog so to speak, it will correspond to when you have the opportunity to pay off this particular new karma. Just a couple of miles up the road someone is squeezing you again in traffic, and to go where you want to go, you would now have to cut off a new person next to you. Realizing you don't want another bad debt, you slow down, losing your ability to make your turn, and having to go past your turn, and drive back around the block just to get back to the route you were on.

What you may not realize is, you have just positively paid or released that newly created karmic debt. By choosing to NOT create a new negative situation, by suffering the long, out of the way route you had to endure, you have just released the previous debt and shown the universe your ability to learn and do the right thing. Going out of your way was the payment for the previous negative attachment and it released the debt. Showing the universe you didn't want to negatively impact another human being, compassion, is your newly created spiritual karma. A win, win situation really and yet many people might just think it was another nuisance created to aggravate their life, force their way in to make the turn, and miss a double opportunity to release and gain karma on two levels.

Earthly karmic debts typically mirror the original negative action, or some derivative like it, so that you show the universe and yourself you have learned from your error in judgment.

Now because you had the opportunity to so quickly pay off this new debt, it represents a sign that you have very little earthly karma stacked up that still needs to be released. How fast things manifest into opportunities to correct them or be rewarded by them shows how close you are to being clean of your earthly karma and or closer to your true self. One who has no negative karma in reserve is very much aligned to their true self and manifests karmic exchanges almost instantly.

Positive earthly karma works the same way. Do a good deed, have a positive thought about someone and you will be rewarded with the same. The world will be your oyster. I have experienced many times a thing I like to call the magical mystery tour. When everything you do, every step you take. The universe opens the door and you move through the day effortlessly and in complete harmony. Only creating new positive earthly and soul karma each and every chance you get. So you pull into the supermarket parking lot and the best space suddenly opens up. That person you were trying to get a hold of suddenly appears before you in the store. That item you need that was so expensive you find out at the check stand is on sale today only………on and on and on it can go. See how long you can keep that going once you fall into it. Athletes in competition call it being in the zone. In daily life I call it the magical mystery tour. See how long you can keep it going before your logical mind gets in the way and says it has to stop. This can't keep happening. Presto, it stops. I once was able to stay on the magical mystery tour for over 3 months. See how long you make it.

    Now let's look at soul or universal karma. We incarnate on earth many times with a very specific soul lesson or lessons in mind. May it be as simple as learning true humility or compassion, or it may be as complex as deciding to change and influence the development of mankind? We then enter into a new body and life as it were, and will carry soul karmic debt from our previous lives as we undertake this new life experience.

Now soul karma influences our daily lives in very powerful ways; both negative and positive. For instance I had been very selfish and had used many people in a negative and almost gluttonous way in my immediately previous life. I had been very successful and had used many people in my rise to that single lifetimes' achievements. Really to no regard as to their own lives and any damage I inflicted on them. But because I had practically cleared all of my own previous karmic soul debt. I was able use my many lifetimes of power almost unabated. Well in my next lifetime I suffered tremendous pain and personal upheaval in my first 21 years in life. A childhood of tremendous personal degradation from both parents, abhorrent violence and constant verbal humiliation. I was unable to escape the abuse as I was having done to me almost exactly what I had done to others in just my previous life.

At 22 my father passed, the largest source of the inflicted negative karma, and suddenly I was released from the bondage of that tumultuous pattern and debt. I literally was reborn and suddenly moved freely to succeed and freely live and enjoy this lifetime like I never thought possible. I won't extrapolate on the karmic conditions that befell my parents in their role of my pain and suffering but we are all willing participants in this dance of karmic debt.

So I seemingly suffered greatly in my formative years but really I was given the gift to pay off my previous negative karmic soul debt of causing other loving caring people to suffer by having it done to me, in the beginning of this lifetime. If I had not accepted the suffering through that time I would still have to carry it into another lifetime, into another set of life circumstances, until the debt was paid AND the spiritual lesson was learned that any attempt to use and manipulate others is not only wrong and inhumane but it incurs tremendous karmic debt.

Soul karma does not rectify or pay off the karmic debt in the same lifetime. A very important concept. That is why we see people doing and creating violence and abuse in present life times and seemingly get away with it without any immediate consequences. That question has been posed by many of how the Creator could allow such violence and injustices to exist. He doesn't. We many times just won't see the full consequences and exchange play out. It could take lifetimes for the soul debt to resurface and the opportunity for the individual to pay off the debt and learn from their previous actions and misunderstandings. And it could take even more lifetimes for the soul to be rewarded for all the positive karma it has acquired and earned at the same time.

You can see as you take millions of people living simultaneously playing out positive and negative soul karmic debts that it can get pretty hard to discern everyone's role and karma propelling their actions and results. Not only was I given the opportunity and chance to give back and do it right in this lifetime, but I was richly rewarded for it.

But you see how suddenly complex our world is to be creating all these debts and payoffs, both positive and negative with all these people running around on planet earth today. Add the complexity of soul karma interwoven with earthly karma and your desire to consciously record and analyze all the inner workings of us living together, and whew, it is mostly incomprehensible to the human brain. Just no way you can hold it all in, The Matrix. The movie is really representational of the code of actions being recorded, the karma and its ramifications. Karma created, released and introduced by all these people, all the time simultaneously. If you look at the computer program of the universe as code you would get the image something like in the movie The Matrix. That's why it has this great universal appeal. It is so close to the truth of the inner makings of the universe.

So take the time to really choose the actions you want to take responsibility for because if you think you are just going to go through life without consequences or reward you are not paying attention. This level of living is supposed to be about realizing our thoughts and actions and that they all have consequences, so do the right thing. Pay attention to your thoughts and actions and take responsibility for them. It will be a grander place for all and an easier path for you.

3 chapter

THE PATH

Move it or lose it

The path is only open to those that are willing to accept a journey.

Stand still on the path of life long enough and you will be mowed over like a semi-truck speeding down the highway. The path of life, as some have stated before, is like a labyrinth. It twists and turns, confuses and be muddles, seemingly going in the wrong direction even at times. It stops, has dead-ends, many times forcing us to backtrack and find a different way. But it always leads to the one and only one final conclusion; Ultimate freedom.

As long as you continue to move and take action, even if as I said it seems to dead-end or backtrack, you will find the exit of the labyrinth which is ultimate freedom.

The labyrinth can be confining and secretive when you are totally immersed in it, hiding its easiest path from plain view. Just like life. You eventually find clues and hints, building memories and guidelines of which ways not to repeat, but if you were able to simply float above the maze you would effortlessly see the simplest way through. It's why the masters are always saying to elevate yourself above the problem and you will see the solution in the simplest way.

Grind, push, hurry to find the exit and you will almost always find you're exhausted and moving in circles, repeating dead-ends and wasting tremendous effort.

So it is a fine balance and an art to find a way to calmly and purposely etch your way along the path of life, always trying to maintain positive movement and balance. And isn't the labyrinth really just a piece of art, much like life should be viewed and embraced. It's complex yet simple, beautiful and impactful, and looked upon and experienced differently by each and every person. Life is a series of artistic expressions and experiences culminating in the highest achievement of ultimate freedom.

Because that is the prize at the end of the journey, the completion of the grand labyrinth, an invitation to exit the lower forms of existence and embrace the final goal of becoming one with the Creator. To return to the Creator's side, which carries with it the greatest gift of all, one's complete spiritual evolution and enlightenment.

As long as you continue to move and take action, even when it seems to dead-end or make you backtrack, you will eventually find the doorway to your inner and outer freedom. As I stated before, the labyrinth of life can be confusing and seemingly secretive but if you find a way to elevate yourself above the maze, out of the blinders that are created, take the time to listen to your soul and its innate guidance, you will receive the wisdom and tools needed to see the way out.

Grow, Live, and Love

We must constantly seek growth in order to live in harmony and balance on Mother Earth.

As we progress from our continual physical growth as a young child, we must seek out a new continual growth in our emerging adulthood. In order for us to maintain our right to live out the full term of each lifetime we must maintain a continuum of spiritual growth. Stall too long on the path of life, try to thwart any new lessons or growth for too long, and you will find yourself, and your physical body, catapulted to the exit door of that lifetime. But you will exit without that prized gift of lessons learned leading to ultimate freedom. Your reward will only be the gift of returning to the beginning of the maze to try it again.

In that, living to the fullest intent, we must seek out love in ourselves and all that lives and breathes around us. To see love embodied in all living things elevates us above the labyrinth in that act of clarity. The walls of the maze will suddenly dissipate leaving only compassion and understanding for all.

We can't confuse others at their own attempts at individual growth as anything other than that. Attempts at growth. They may exhibit greed, selfishness, anger, or just plain confusion and it all originates from their desire to grow, to find that ultimate freedom for themselves. It just gets distorted in their own impatience or fear that maybe they won't in fact find their freedom because they can't see it. Unsure if they are going to be able to find the exit. They certainly are lost or they wouldn't act that way.

An illusion as you know but we see it manifested every day in various forms all around us. My favorite is those that try to buy their salvation or exit from the maze. The only thing that they ending up purchasing is an invitation to try one more time, start over again at the mouth of the labyrinth, or the beginning of a new lifetime.

If we embody this ever expanding love to all that is, we will and do, achieve that ultimate growth, that ultimate goal. The growth of the soul, the completion of the labyrinth and all the wisdom, peace, and serenity that comes along with it.

Grow, Live, and Love

We must Grow in order to Live.
We must Live in order to Love.
We must Love in order to Grow.

And most importantly we must love ALL in order to experience the miracles of life.

There is no right path, no wrong path, no I must be on someone else's path, I can't see the path, or for surely not; why don't I ever seem to be on the right path. There is only one path. If you wake up in the morning and you are alive, you are on the path, your path, unique and individualized, and created by you and the Creator to facilitate your ability to balance your karma and soul in order to facilitate your constant spiritual evolution.

You may feel like your progress has become stagnant, you may feel like you're going backwards on the path. But believe me, every second of every minute of every day on earth, you are on your path. You just may not be realizing the complexities and diversities the path, your path, has to take in order for you to complete your journey forward.

The Egyptians embraced the snake symbol throughout their culture with its adornment in jewelry, woven in fabric, present in their hieroglyphics, and most noteworthy in their grand headdresses on their kings and queens. It was their definition of the path, their symbolism of it. They believed it signified the road you had to travel on the path of life. Not a straight easily definable line, but a deliberate winding ever-changing route or progression, best symbolized by the snake in its body of coils as it moves forward in its intention.

So take the time to realize that whatever is happening in your life, you are on the right path. You just haven't been given the clarity yet to see the benefits of the situation and its intended outcome. Ask for guidance from your soul and allow it to present itself.

Seek illumination on your confusion and if your soul does not respond immediately, release it and the answer will come to you in due time. Many times understanding the outcome of a situation before hand would greatly impede our desire and learning ability essential to the progress on the path.

Remember to always finish what you start in your life so that your journey, while many times circuitous, will continually lead you forward to the glory of ultimate freedom and the attainment of complete spiritual enlightenment

4 chapter

Homemade Soup

Learning how to take our daily medicine

Intention, Intention, *Intentions*. Any medicine or remedy worth its salt has to be made with the greatest intention. To love and embrace the individual and to prompt the soul to heal is essential. Take chicken soup, the greatest cure-all ever known to modern man. Mom painstakingly stands over a hot stove adding just the right combinations of ingredients, chicken, vegetables, spices, and her own special touch – love. Doggone no holds barred serving of motherly love. Right there in a bowl the single most important ingredient needed to heal the sick. How many radiation treatments, chemotherapy drugs, and expansive antibiotics have this one essential ingredient or intention?

You know the answer so I don't have to say it. But what are we to do when we have been presented with only these options and nothing else? Refuse lifesaving chemical compounds and let our child or loved one suffer in agony. Stand idly by and watch then contend with dying without helping them? Well, let's backtrack a little before we have to address the extreme illnesses.

It all started when we stopped honoring our responsibility to always respect and embrace anything and everything we put in our body. Whatever happened to the act of giving thanks before every meal? It doesn't have to be bombastic or complicated, just honor the fact that some living breathing thing, animal and or vegetable gave their life for you. So that you could go on living breathing and hopefully evolving. Return to that simple moment of giving thanks before each meal and realize how quickly and differently we will view and choose our consumption.

Eating fast food, shoving meals down our throat as we rush to get somewhere, agonizing over what little time we have to eat, and hurrying to wolf down the food in order to catch our favorite TV re-run is all damaging and with mistaken intention. To rush to get it over with will only result in failure for the body to accept the intended healing properties. Whenever your body has a negative reaction to a food, a drug, and or a therapy, not only is it reacting to the wrong source being ingested, but it is reacting to the wrong intention in which it was created, delivered, and introduced into the body.

The source and preparation of the food always has an incredible impact on its success as a healing agent. As well as the state of mind in which we prepare and consume the meal. Even when we have a home cooked meal if we think we really didn't have the time to make it or no one seemed to enjoy it, it negates the act and purpose of the meal. It has a negative impact on its ability to heal or properly regentrify the soul, our energy, and the physical body.

We miss the opportunity – we have the wrong intention. And our bodies, our soul, and the future of our health pay the price. Maybe not right away but the accumulative effect can be devastating.

Remember when we couldn't drive through some food shack to get our meals. We had to make the time to plan our meals, to stock the needed foods, and to calculate the needs of our body in advance. We had to stop our daily lives and think "What do I want to eat tomorrow, and the next day, and what sounds good for the day after that". Actually connecting to ourselves, our soul, and our natural sense of what is needed to move forward in our lives and maintain a healthy life. All necessary to creating a positive intention that translates to good food, good habits, and healthy living.

There is still a glimmer of that natural balance and communication that resides in our self. When you still make your list to go to the grocery store for what little you may or may not still prepare for yourself and family, you can catch yourself thinking "Well I did have steak or meat every day last week, maybe I should try some fish. I keep reading it's good to be eating more of it". That communication, that awareness and intention is essential to good health. Not, I have 8 minutes to rush to the next meeting or whatever other silly commitment you have agreed to, and I'll just quickly stop and pick something up. Then when we are in a rush and not clear of our healthy needs, and certainly not with any overview of our whole natural consumptions, we pick the thing that might taste good, quickly, absent minded, and blindly. And we certainly don't stop to add love into our happy meal before devouring into our now destructing vessel.

Even more detrimental is the intention of this so-called meal. The energy, the negative intention injected by the malcontent, doesn't want to be there "I hate my life" cook preparing our meal. The unnaturally raised, drug injected, violently sacrificed meat and dead vegetable bomb we try to call a meal.

Even fine dining can make us ill given again the intention of the purchased food, the complimentary ingredients, and the simple mood and *intention* of the chef that day. We may not all have had gourmet cooks as Moms but they all carried the one essential ingredient – Love. Mom's food never looked so good until you break it down and realize that intentions are everything.

The intention of the grower; greed, self-profit, or wanting to help and feed people in a healthy way.

That will guide his every decision as he raises the animals or produces his crops. Does he use destructive unnatural chemicals to induce more product, more greed, or does he spare no cost or efforts to ensure the healthiness and vitality of the products? This is the impact of the first stage of growing the food and already it could be ruined before it even gets on the truck to go to market. The average food on the shelf in America today has traveled 1,200 miles to get to our modern stores, how's that for destructive. Live food my eye. It only gets multiplied and compounded in a negative fashion with this current system.

There are so many variables that can reduce the quality and natural healing qualities of mass- produced, mass-distributed, and mass-prepared food, I could keep writing for pages. Just understand that it is a domino of counterproductive actions that keep feeding and creating our ever blossoming illnesses.

So called modern medicines have an entirely different complexity to them. Not only have most been produced and generated with only greed in mind, they try to cure the illnesses by bypassing the needed mutual participation necessary to really heal an individual that has created this dis-ease. Note I did not say contracted I said created. We are the creators of everything in our life including our illnesses. The lessons needing to be embraced and the changes that have to happen before someone is truly healed, are thwarted by the modern drugs intention to circumvent that process and directly manipulate the physiological make-up of the body and its condition. It many times just makes it worse.

Now we live in a new age that has bred new advanced pathogens and diseases that would not exist with a natural and balanced planet. So I have to give credence to the fact that modern drugs can be useful. Particularly when someone is awoken in a diseased state that is very advanced and especially life threatening. The modern drugs and therapies can and will stem the proliferation and wide spreading illness so its usage can be very important. But it cannot, and should not be the end all or looked upon as the cure. It is only the beginning of the work that will be needed in order to solve and promote change in the individual that is necessary for them to be healed once and for all.

Why do you think dis-eases keep coming back to people, or mutate into another form of illness just a little bit later. They forgot to do the work, make the changes, and furthermore realize that they brought this on themselves to learn and grow from it. The modern drugs and therapies let them escape that responsibility and awareness.

Now I know, why would a seven year old create cancer in themselves, what error or direction could they be ignoring, how could they be struck down on their path when their life has just begun? Remember that major illnesses almost always are past life related. Its karma from another lifetime being exchanged in this life time. Not only that but there are lessons learned by the individual and those around them that are so profound and so impactful that it really is easy to comprehend the importance of the illness. It is a seemingly tragic diagnosis that we usually are only able to embrace for pain and not for the gifts.

Be careful of what you eat. Acknowledge why you are eating it and for what purpose. Pay close attention to your body as it will communicate accurately what you should be consuming on a daily basis in order to stay healthy and in balance. Most importantly any dis-ease you are revealed to have needs to be addressed at the soul level, the karmic level, and the needed understanding that many solutions and changes will be necessary for you to properly heal yourself once and for all. That you must take an active role in your healing and that your willing participation is the single most important element in the mix.

No one can truly heal another; we can only help those to heal themselves through many different ways, remedies, and opportunities. Doctors aren't wrong in dispensing drugs; they can be some of the most loving, compassionate people you will ever meet. They just have become blinded by the pressures in our modern society to erase our cries of discomfort. They have simply forgotten their responsibility to shepherd us down the true road of recovery and not to try to wipe out our dis-ease for us.

5 chapter

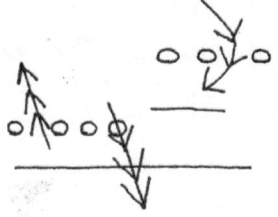

Quantum Physical

Understanding the inner workings of all bodies

The physical body has been analyzed and scrutinized by modern science ad nauseam. And I only say that because for as much as they claim to understand all of its inner workings they refuse to give credence to the other, ethereal, and planetary bodies living in existence that constantly influence each other on a daily basis. Sure they recognize that the earth is alive in some way but not to the extent that it is breathing, thinking, and functioning as intricate and complex as the human body does.

Whereby the ethereal body is completely ignored. Which is incredible for it animates and regulates all of the functions of the physical body moment by moment. Fix the energy flow of an individual and you can heal the physical body almost instantaneously. Eastern culture and its healing practices completely understand this connection and have created the beautiful healing ways of acupuncture and acupressure for the benefit of its entire people. But western medicine only tolerates the existence of the eastern understandings and refuses to really embrace it in any useful way. It would be so easy to have both modalities harmoniously integrated, working in concert so as to best prevent and help people in the most non-intrusive and natural way. But I digress.

    The physical body is the last in the train of connections and actions created by our mental and soul level decisions. It is the first to be abandoned in crisis and the only one of the bodies left to decay and die when our soul has decided to continue onward to the learning on higher levels of existence. Planets are still kept alive, souls are forever, and the ethereal body reemerges into a different shell transforming with our soul on other planes that we move to after our life, or lives on earth.

    The physical body suffers the most damage of any negative energy we create and manifest, and it retains the emotional vehicle entwined in its make-up that does not exist in our soul. Past life remembrance is without emotional memory. It is only when we would incarnate back into a new life that we would associate any past life memories with emotions.

Mother Earth does have an emotional heart string but it does not resonate in negative perpetuity as it forgives all that is done to her in her grand understanding of universal compassion. Not the body. Just get near someone or something from your past that has hurt you and your body goes into overdrive. Sparking adrenaline, nervous reactions, physical illness, and just flat out mayhem. What a mess.

That's why most people who have past life remembrances, or retain the dying memory in a lifetime, recall that the minute they leave the body they are overwhelmed with the sensation of incredible peace and serenity. Not burning anxiety of where am I going next, what will happen to my possessions, or even what about my loved ones. Just a sense of incredible calmness and freedom.

The physical body is built to teach us that we can control how things are viewed and how they can affect us, our soul. How we can create positive responses and actions no matter what happens in life, or succumb to the negative thoughts and all the destruction that it creates. A direct cause and effect, an incredible teaching tool. But that is all that it is, a teaching tool. not, let me repeat that, NOT anything more than a teaching tool. Certainly not a complete reality on any true higher level of understanding.

Take for example that you are involved in a horrific car accident. Your body suffers massive injuries and trauma. In this car accident your arm is severed and you feel incredible pain and suffering. You linger a little while you try to stay alive but then you die shortly thereafter from sustaining these life threatening injuries. Now you would pass effortlessly to the next dimension where you would suddenly realize your soul is still completely intact. And your complete ethereal body is also still in one piece. So did you really lose your real arm, a part of your soul and ethereal body? No, you damaged and mangled, quite well I might add, the physical shell you inhabited and now had to abandon it. You left it on the side of the road, just like your car, after the accident destroyed both your car and your physical earth body. So was the pain real? Sure was intense, at least it seemed like at the time. But did you cause any real damage and injury to the things that make up your true self, your soul and ethereal body? Absolutely damage was done, again blood, guts, body parts everywhere you looked, but your soul and ethereal body was untouched. *You* were untouched. So physical pain and suffering is only real to the extent that you choose to accept it in its limitations. On the physical plane and inhabited in a physical shell. And on what level of existence you choose to determine reality is to the extent that you can realize the true magnitude of that statement.

The ethereal body as I have stated a few times now, animates the physical. Puppeteers its movements and impacts its reactions. Great feats of strength have occurred with a person's ability to extrapolate large amounts of raw energy in short bursts to what is only characterized as super human powers. So it can magnify the normal day to day physical abilities and movements, but it mostly just moves the strings of the body as the mind and emotions desire in a natural continuous way.

Emotions are also attached to the ethereal as long as you reside in a physical body. Double whammy so to speak. That's why emotional experiences can lower or raise your energy level and in turn heighten or lower your physical responses. Kind of a dual catalyst so to speak.

Now energy as explained in the first chapter is created by the ignition of life-force through the inner flame present in your body. It can also be added to by accepting the universal flow of energy through chakras present in the ethereal body. There are seven major Chakras and 4 minor Chakras. The seven major chakras are commonly known as; the crown chakra (top of the head), the third eye Chakra (just above the nose between the eyes), the throat chakra (right in the middle of your Adams apple), the heart chakra (middle of the heart), the solar plexus chakra (just below the sternum), the sacral chakra (2 inches under center of your belly button), and the root or bottom chakra (right below your rectum). The four minor chakras are in the centers of your palms and almost center on the bottom of each foot. These are less known but very powerful. It's were people do hand energy healing and how you can ground your energy into the earth for more power and balance. There are many books available on the chakra system so I won't go into too much detail on them for it really can take a whole book to explain them.

The important quick summary though is as follows: You can gain new pure energy for strength or healing by opening up and receiving through your crown (top chakra). Wisdom and guidance can be accepted and given in energy thought form through your third eye chakra. Your feelings and thought energies are released through your throat chakra when you communicate.

When you stuff your verbal expressions and emotions you clog your throat chakra, which eventually leads to physical dis-ease and illness. Usually around and including the throat. Simply shutting down any of the major chakras leads to tremendous imbalance and leads to minor and then major illness. Almost always directly correlative to that area in the body. Shut down the heart chakra and you will develop heart complications and disease. Shut down the solar plexus chakra and you develop stomach problems and eventually organ breakdowns. You can see the physical connections as you study the purposes of the chakras and their intentions.

You heart chakra is the big kahuna. Receiving and giving through it is the basis of loving, caring, and living. You must have it open and flowing so as to keep your spiritual balance and growth alive. And you must be able to receive through it in order to satisfy your soul and all of your bodily components. Shut down your heart chakra and shut down your LIFE. Trauma and life pain has a tendency to shut it down, a natural and acceptable response, but never allow it to stay closed for too long for the consequences are grave. That's how seemingly simple and innocuous statements can have so much truth and power, and understanding – Keep your heart always open.

The solar plexus chakra while having emotions and feelings expressed through it has its major importance with being the center of your outward flow of energy. As you take in extra universal energy, or other people's energy, you have to balance the amount of energy in your etheric body. That is best regulated by the solar plexus chakra. You can release extra or even negative energy by opening up and releasing the energy out through it. A great healing meditation is to draw white light, pure healing energy in through the top of our head (crown chakra) and let it flow down through our entire ethereal body, to our toes and back up and out our solar plexus chakra. Keeping the rhythm in tandem to our inhaling and exhaling breath. Get overwhelmed by someone's energy and you can release it back out through your solar plexus to keep your balance.

The last two chakras, the sacral and the root, both involve sexual energy, intimacy, and most emotions that we take in and exchange. To have your heart chakra fully open, these chakras also have to be open and flowing otherwise your heart will never open up completely to its needed expanse. When you sense someone is untrue or without proper intention you will feel it through your sacral chakra, thus the gut feeling. When you feel ungrounded or flighty you have closed off your root chakra and no longer have energy flowing to Mother Earth and the positive benefits of being grounded to her.

So much to discover in just the seven major and minor chakras. There are also 17 spiral chakras that revitalize your energy flow; it is the basis for the main meridians in acupuncture. There also exists additional sub chakras that are present in the body to access large filters that reside in the ethereal body and can be momentarily taken out, cleaned and put back. It is a direct replicate idea of the filter system in our physical body. Like the body we take in toxins, negative energy, and it must be constantly filtered out in order to keep the ethereal body healthy and flowing. It must also be flowing in proper directions and at a constant proper rate. Many healers can utilize some or all of these different accesses to the energy body to facilitate healing and cleansing.

We have ethereal umbilical cords attached to our back that keeps us constantly connected to other people and their energy. We have invited other people to create this connection and can constantly feel and monitor them as much or as little as we like. Unfortunately they can draw and steal energy and even life force from us with this ethereal umbilical attachment. So we really shouldn't be letting people get this deep into our beings. It happens with intimacy and exchanges of any deep or impactful emotional exchange.

Good energy healers can rectify these potentially exhaustive and detrimental attachments in order for us to see and exist with only our own energy at play.

The planets and specifically Mother Earth have an energy body like our own and constantly accept and give out these productive and counterproductive vibrations. They are in tune to negative and positive impulses even more than we will admit, so you have to recognize the power of your thoughts, the power of the life and influence of the planets, and how we all impact each other.

Native culture explains that while they migrated north and south as the seasons and weather dictated more harmonious living conditions, they also describe that we as people needed to leave the ground in which we resided on for the earth to cleanse and re-gentrify were we had impression-ed our energy and life experiences into it. Keeping constant movement seems to be always a theme in some way or another.

So as you can see, we have great influence on the health and welfare of our physical, ethereal, and yes, even planetary bodies we inhabit. We must continue to participate and constantly move forward in order for it all to survive in balance and harmony. Our desire to shirk our acceptance of this influence has been an attempt to lessen our responsibilities and understandings which has created the present circumstances where we have forgotten the abilities and rewards of the universe. If we return to these understandings we will be able to embrace the completeness that will go along with a little extra effort and that total recognition.

chapter 6

Systematic Breakdown

The impact of negative energy

In order for us to evolve into our true higher selves we many times must have, what I call, a complete systematic breakdown of our core. It is the tearing down and restructuring of our lives and cellular structure. Calamity and overall general mayhem overtakes many, and or all, aspects of our lives. This happens in order for us to be able to see the obstacles we have created and how they are impeding our spiritual evolution. It also enables the cellular structure an opportunity to reassemble, or repair the damage that has been created in the formation of such negative imbalances.

When everything is going along smoothly we have no motivation to analyze or re-evaluate our life. It is only when general disintegration of our everyday life happens that we stop long enough to potentially re-evaluate anything happening to and around us. Many times we have to attract a major illness or seemingly tragic event in order for us to introduce change that brings us to a new beginning and spiritual advancement.

Out of chaos comes clarity. The ordering of our system, beliefs, and energetic structures that we hold to be true in this particular lifetime. A reshuffling of the deck you might say.

Like a dog that has fleas, we have to shake and scratch our souls, so to speak, in order to expose these energetic parasites and their strong hold. For example Mother Earth is constantly creating earthquakes, floods, fires, and storms in order to cleanse and facilitate the clearing of its building or stagnant negative energies.

The severity of earth changes is relative to the magnitude of the accumulating negative energy. Much like dreams whereas the fullness of the impact of the dream is equal to the severity of the message. What and when do we most remember our dreams? When we get frightened or scared out of wits, then we remember the dream. Nightmares, we always remember nightmares. We are many times even woken up in the middle of a nightmare because they are so impactful and important.

The masters taught me that the magnitude of the dream is directly relative to the importance of the message. Dreams are our unconscious mind re-evaluating our spiritual progress on a daily basis. And when simple dreams are not listened to; a gentle reminder of what to focus on in our daily life, our subconscious mind conjures up a nightmare to really get our attention. Shaking the soul or scratching at the fleas. And if we have a reoccurring nightmare, well suffice it say we are really not listening to our soul about something really, really important.

Same with earth changes, same with calamity in our life. The soul is asking for your attention to a very important issue impeding your spiritual growth. The earth changes occur as we as a collective soul group are negating and refusing to accept spiritual evolution as a whole, with ourselves and with the planet.

Mother Earth is going to evolve, with our without us. In one of my pilgrimages to the

Mayan temple of Tikal I spent the day with a great Mayan elder who described the coming earth changes as exactly that. Man's recent inability and refusal to listen to and respect Mother Earth. Because of that it will result in her shaking all of the fleas, modern man and his negative conditions, off her back in a great cleansing. If fleas bite a dog long enough and hard enough, he will find a way to rid the parasites of their invasion. And that's what negative energy does to us, our spiritual evolution, and Mother Earth. It irritates and pokes at our natural balance long enough and consistently enough to finally create a systematic breakdown.

Systemic release is the direct result of systematic breakdown. Read that carefully. *Systemic* release is the direct result of systematic breakdown. As the negative energy breaks down the internal organisms it expands and contracts, building to a point where it has to seek release so as not to fracture the physical cellular structure.

The magma of the center of Mother Earth builds and expands in a conductive response to the negative energy impacting and propagating on its surface and in the solar system. Pollution, greed, and destruction of natural resources, all create negative magnification of the impact on the nucleus of the earth until it causes an earthquake, torrential storms, or even greater, volcanic eruptions. All signals for man to change and start mitigating his creation of negative energy. When he does not heed the message, Mother Earth has no choice but to seek a major release and clearing of the negative energies and their creative force.

As history has shown us, many times it is man that has been responsible for these systematic breakdowns more than the celestial influences. Man in his denial of his influence of Mother Earth and his impacts of his negative cultural de-evolution, ignores her warning signs and pays the price. In even a few extreme cases creating scenarios in which he is almost completely wiped out. Thus the reason for the breakdown and loss of a few major and once great and flourishing civilizations.

The body in its synergistic mirror of Mother Earth goes through similar and many times simultaneous breakdowns in order to reconfigure the energies to a new and healthy state of balance. The disrupted makeup of the cellular structure begins a new pattern of movement on the etheric or energy plane.

There are 3 etheric or energy cells for every physical cell in the body. In a healthy state they have a clockwise centrifugal movement. When negative energy disrupts the balance of the etheric body, the etheric cells begin a new pattern of movement, in turn negatively influencing the physical cell. Instead of maintaining a centrifugal force, necessary to healthy conductivity, the etheric cells stop circling the physical cells and begin to bounce or bombard the individual cell. They begin an elastic bombardment, breaking up the single physical cell into smaller multiple cells. Modern science sees it as massive cellular reproduction but it really is the dividing or fracturing of the cell into a compilation of newer unbalanced cells.

Not only is the mass production of original cells stuck in the craze of the bombardment, they are eventually abandoned by the etheric cells and left isolated in that unstabilized state. The ultimate death of the multiplied newer cells is inevitable. They have been distorted in such a way that they are unable to be properly action-ed ever again by the etheric cells. Leaving behind a mass of dead cell growth and fungal debris, a tumor or growth, and ultimately what modern science diagnoses as cancer and just plain out and out carnage.

Not only is oxygen one of the first two original components of the universe but it is the fuel for the centrifugal etheric force. That's why no disease can survive in a state of pure oxygen. It fuels and reconstitutes the centrifugal force of the etheric cells. It basically reinstates balance and the re-gentrification of the now dis-eased cells to a healthy state. That's why oxygen chambers, oxygen induced waters, and any oxygen enhancing medicines like colloidal silver are incredible remedies. They represent almost a magic healing for most dis-ease and nonperforming cellular structures.

As we head to a new age we will begin to understand many more healing principles and therapies but the real importance is to listen to the warning signs of our soul, the planet, and every living thing that we interact with. To wait until we have such drastic systematic breakdown and such painful systemic releases before we make changes, has to be getting old and tiresome. Not listening to the information available is to continue on a course of constant destruction and rebuilding, which has no place in the new configuration of our new age.

7 chapter

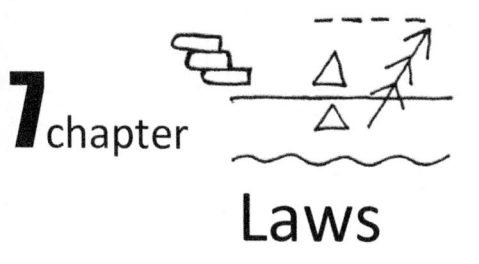

Laws

How to know when you are about to be pulled over

There are seven major universal laws. The granddaddies of universal laws you might say. There were originally twelve but man in his defeat of not wanting to having to live in a garden of Eden – or a multiple dimensional world without negative consequences as a guide, abandoned the later five; Truth, Justice, Mercy, Salvation, and Illumination. He instead exchanged them for the law of Karma which is embodied in the seventh still existing major law of compassion.

In man's discontent to live, grow, and move throughout multiple dimensions at will, He chose instead to create an isolated beginning level of learning; life on earth. There he believed he would be more stringently guided by the law and ramifications of Karma to facilitate his initial journeys towards spiritual enlightenment. Whereas the karmic condition creates the acceptance of whatever man has in his thoughts, they in turn create and control the destiny of his world here on earth. Whatever he thinks he creates, both negative and positive. Great learning tool if you embrace its powerful simplicity.

    The existing seven major laws are fairly simple and self-illuminating if you just take the time to meditate on them. They are the laws of Order, Balance, Harmony, Growth, Creator Perception, Love, and Compassion.

    The law of Order is meant mostly for the order of the mind. When chaos or confusion envelopes the mind it creates chaos and destruction of our lives and body. Keep your thoughts clear, positive, and consistent, and you will quickly be in complete control of your life and the things that manifest in it. Let your mind continually churn, mull over different possibilities, and never let it be quiet in its decisions and you will create so much inner and outer conflict it will be debilitating. You will quickly believe that you are only a reaction to a seemingly disarray of uncontrollable events.

The law of Balance embodies the idea that whatever you create, desire and experience must have a natural balance to it. Too much or too little of anything will always create a correction of things to reinstate a balance. You can create the necessities of life, food, shelter, clothing but you must also balance those manifestations with the creation of opportunities and experiences that equally promote your spiritual evolution. Too much material creation and not enough spiritual development will quickly ignite the scales of balance to supersede.

Now don't ever misinterpret the law of Balance in a way that makes you believe that you have to suffer in life as much as you have the right to enjoy it. You can experience daily exhilaration without owing any suffering in exchange. Suffering is neither an inherent concept nor a necessity; it is only a lower vibration tool for education and karmic debt payment chosen by each individual for his own purpose and advancement.

The law of Harmony is the vibrational condition that exists in ourselves, all of nature, and the entire universe. The intent of recognizing and embracing that Creator essence, that giver of life that can be felt at all times in all things. To embrace the ocean, to immerse yourself in the earth, and to subtract yourself from the limited expression of materialism, is to connect to the harmony of our life-force and all its expansion and existence in all things. A constant hum or vibration of all living things. Connect to that on a daily basis and you will embrace the harmony of life, the harmony of your soul and all things around us.

    The law of Growth is clearly defined in Chapter 3 "The Path". We have an undeniable responsibility to constantly seek growth or movement towards the return of our union with the Creator. To become one with the All in All as they say. To consistently and vigilantly work and focus towards that goal and its progress.

    The law of Creator Perception is a very shamanistic concept whereby you are constantly in awe at the beauty and wonderment of the creations of the universe and the Creator. The incredible colors and fragrance of the flowers, the majestic grandeur of the mountains and sky. A continual appreciation and respect for all things that exist and interact with us and around us in our daily lives on Mother Earth. See the beauty and feel the magnitude of the design and creation. Don't just stop and smell the flowers, take the time to reflect in reverence of this grand creation that we are all privileged to live in and grow in, that is all around us.

The law of Love is obvious but so easily cast aside. Without giving love you have no life. Without receiving love you cannot live. Without seeking love in everything around us our life withers and dies before our very eyes. Love is the key to all that was created and it is the solution to any great mystery or problem. Find yourself stuck in any scenario and encircle it with love. It will resolve itself. No negative condition can survive when it is embraced by love. It has to evolve or move away. If only we reached for love whenever we needed a solution, the world would be so much simpler, and so much greater.

The law of Compassion is easy to understand and yet the hardest to maintain and agree to in a consistently balanced manner. We can easily be compassionate for animals and children but the guy who has everything we think hardly deserves our compassion. Yet he probably is the mostly likely to need it. To have compassion at all times, to turn the other cheek and forgive and understand all seemingly abhorrent and selfish acts is so hard to do, but so easily understood that it needs no further explanation.

What we need is the determination not to succumb to any other decisions or reactions but compassion, especially for our fellow man. Karma is the tool that constantly reminds us of when we don't choose compassion as the solution to our life and its problems. Have compassion all the time and you will wipe out any negative karmic condition you have ever had. It will also build new positive karma, something we could all use more of.

There are many more laws and sub structure concepts that influence our lives and evolution in addition to the seven major universal laws.

The law of Manifestation, whatever you desire, dream of having or creating, you can manifest in your life. Yes I said everything. You are not given the desire for something without being given the opportunity to manifest it. All of your desires here on earth can and will manifest, given enough time and continued positive consistent thought. I want this, no now I want that, no, no, I didn't really want that. If you are ever wondering why things are taking so long for your desires to manifest, then you need to re-evaluate your thought process. You have to be very strict in your thoughts or wandering thoughts, and ever changing thoughts.

You are always given the opportunity in your life for all your desires to manifest into reality. The caveats that come into play are clarity of thought and karmic debt. Karma is forever entwined with manifestation and must be realized so as not to endure lost efforts.

Win the lottery as you desire but still owe a large karmic debt which necessitates the loss of money and hardship to pay off, and you lose the lottery winnings in a flash. Now maybe you may have chosen to learn humility in this lifetime and that experience can also help teach you humility. It is just that by losing everything you just gained is a lot of wasted effort. And in what is a highly emotional and impactful scenario that didn't have to play out in such a denigrating way. It's so hard to win everything and then just lose it all again in a moment. You could have learned the lesson of humility, paid the karmic debt, all in a gentler and less emotional series of situations than the one you had created with say, the lottery scenario.

The complexity of the inner workings of our newly formed desires in a lifetime, our individual goals we set out to achieve in our spiritual evolution of each lifetime, and the scenarios in which they all come together into our present reality, can all be very, very intricate. That's why you can't try to control life because frankly you just can't even begin to comprehend how much effort and intricacy is necessary in the creation process for every new moment and event to take place. That's why a great affirmation for manifestation for what you want within harmonic balance is to ask the universe for help in manifesting your desires in the perfect way. There are many, many powerful and insightful books available today which are fantastic for shepherding you in this great principle or law.

But I digress as usual and only want to illustrate to you that you need to ask your inner self for guidance when you manifest things so that events happen in harmony and balance with your karma and spiritual progression. It will help in finding a way to minimize all this undue strife and downright agony that frankly was never the intention of this great planet and its educational vehicle.

But remember you can have anything you desire, anything you think of you can manifest. Don't ever let anyone lead you to believe otherwise.

Law of Attraction. I had this woman recently that came to me and complained that a person in their life just won't leave her alone, won't go away no matter what she does. This person, she sees it, is creating tremendous havoc and unnecessary pain in her life. She asked me: "How do I get rid of this other person? What do I have to do?" I said maybe you owe them something. And she said: "I never met them before". To which I replied: "How do you know? Do you remember everything and every person from the past say 500 years worth of lifetimes you may have had?" And she replied "Of course not, who does". And I said "Then how do you know you don't owe them something, or they owe you? They've probably come to settle the debt between you that you created and actualized many lifetimes ago. They just showed up, in this lifetime, at this moment, and you don't remember your previous agreement".

Don't turn away from an opportunity to honor a karmic debt, a spiritual lesson, just because you don't remember making it. It appears because it is necessary to resolve it in order for the both of you to be able to move forward into new relationships and new successes.

Knowing when you are about to be pulled over refers to the understanding of being aware enough not to ignore our responsibility in recognizing the laws of the universe that exist.

There are many, many more that you can find and educate yourself about. Acknowledging that we are bound and invoking laws and their ramifications, positive and negative, each and every day will help alleviate much of the daily confusion and surprise that we mostly easily could do without. It symbolizes that it is better to accept that greater responsibility that we do create everything that happens in our life and not to be the victim of these seemingly non related events that we say we have no control over.

Speed down the highway of life, ignoring and impacting the laws of the universe, and you will get pulled over. Pretending you didn't know there were laws, and you will just make it worse.

Chapter 8

Alchemy

Tools to survive going forward

The Alchemist story throughout history tells a tale whereby he was able to transform common metal into gold. A great skill if you possess it, but it has only been understood as an urban myth so to speak; until now. Ormus, an ancient known form of white gold, has recently been re-discovered along with a few other new strange compounds. It suddenly has people wondering whether or not we really do have any concept of what really exists in this world and what is possible. Have we even scratched the surface of what science has tried to define as all there is? We have been told that there are only this many elements, only these kinds of metals, and just 12 planets, and only one galaxy. So many of these misconceptions are suddenly being reworked and will be retracted as we accelerate exponentially into this new age. It is only the beginning of the sudden realization that there exists many, many, many, useful and once forgotten powerful tools that will transform our lives in the coming years.

Why have we been blinded by science? Well it comforts our need to believe that we have to have a complete understanding of all that can influence us so that we don't have to walk around with the knowledge or fear that unforeseen elements can suddenly disrupt our seemingly protected and secure lives. Who's afraid of the bogeyman? Everyone, so we teach our young and ourselves that there is no unseen forces in existence and that comforts us and allows us to go back to sleep.

Well, sleep no longer for the only way to survive through the coming changes and the new age is to open ourselves up to the vast sea of unseen forces that have always existed and are now being reawakened and acknowledged.

Granted the movement in our galaxies and the re-positioning of our planet in the solar system is bringing about the greater availability for the harmonic and vibrational shifts to occur.

They are necessary in order to realize and utilize these once lost powers and elements.

That's why the Mayan calendar stops at 2012. Not because it is the end of civilization or this planet, it is the end of our world as we have known it. The greatest astronomers of recently recorded history knew that we would be entering into a new part of the galaxy, new configurations and influences that they themselves had not yet witnessed nor understood. Their highly advanced tools of astronomy and mathematical hypotheses that had illuminated and guided them so well could not venture forward into this new unforeseen galaxy that we are now entering. Thus the end of the current calendar and the end of life as we once understood it.

In better terms the beginning of a new age and a new set of tools and possibilities that will truly change life on earth as never before. Exciting, you bet, frightening, I don't know. It all depends on how tightly you're strapped in before the rocket launch, the accelerated change.

Our bodies have been adjusting for over a decade now and you should be getting used to the new energies and influences or guaranteed the ride will be bumpy. Take time to feel the cellular change and adjust and embrace it. Don't think you're crazy for feeling totally different these days. You should feel different if you are at all paying attention to what is going on. We can't expect to understand everything that is happening to us but we can take comfort in knowing that it is happening to everyone. Some are just more sensitive and more vocal than others.

Within a couple of years we will be able to re gentrify almost every part of our physical body. Heal each other easily and openly as if it were always common place. Naturally and within our own understanding. We will be able to grow new teeth, re-grow severed limbs, naturally regenerate major organs, and basically eliminate all illnesses. Even communicate freely without words. We will be able to do almost anything and everything we had once deemed science fiction in our writings in this recent modern society.

The only problem is that as an individual you will have to allow your mind and cellular structure to evolve to a higher consciousness in order to facilitate these abilities. The destructive behaviors and selfish attitudes of the soon to be past will need to be replaced with the elevated thinking and attitudes of compassion, and harmony, and love. The universal laws that we once have so easily abandoned for this present convoluted modern society must be re-embraced.

We have to begin to be responsible for all that we consume and interact with in our life. We must begin to investigate and understand how to grow our own food, make our own medicines and remedies, and even filter or generate our own water. It is not because the world is ending and we must all run for the hills, it is because we have given up our own genius required to evolve to higher understandings. If we accept that we can all rediscover our own abilities to nurture, replenish, and heal our own bodies, we will rejoin the journey of the Alchemist that is so essential to this new coming age.

We were able to do this many civilizations ago, we just regressed in reaction to the over abundant power that we failed to respect in those times. In a return to a simpler life we gave up our recognition of our own innate power and knowledge. We fell asleep in our own evolution thinking it would rectify the errors of our past. We can no longer stay shrouded in our wisdom and recognition of all that exists and can be empowered in our daily lives on this planet.

    Start your inner change now and realize that not only will we change as a planet, re-embracing all the ancient knowledge, secrets, and gifts that come with it, but we will be rewarded with the complete elimination of all dis-ease and the pain and unnecessary turmoil it has perpetrated on our past civilizations. Open your heart and expand your mind for the new age is beginning and you won't be disappointed, just amazed.

9 chapter

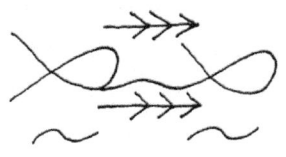

Ascended Living

Grow, Live, and Love

There is a continuity of life that is ever revolving yet continually changing. Ascended living – Grow, Live, and Love. As we rise above to the other levels of planetary existence we begin to embrace all that is necessary to exist within the expression that is the purity of our originating life force, the All in All, the Creator of all things. We begin to see the limited concepts that shroud our brain on this lowest level of life on planet earth.

I asked the Creator one day "Don't you ever do anything anymore?" To which he replied "I already did everything I could". "But then why do you let all the problems, disease, and pain and suffering continue to exist" I prodded. "I do not" he said, and after a slight pause he uttered "Man's freewill". And that was it, the Creator's grand illumination to me one day, my one big conversation with the All in All. It was mans' choice to create karmic debt in order for him to gauge his progression to his return of his original form, the goal to be reunited with the Creator.

There is no pain, no suffering in the memory of the soul of each individual. There is only awareness of his journey and lessons as he seeks the highest level of understanding of all that embodies the universe.

In ascended living we begin to realize that each individual is seeking the same purpose. To better himself or herself, to create and experience fully the lessons that are presented to us each and every day. Participate again and again, until we learn to truly grow, live, and love. I know I keep repeating myself but it is worthy of constant repetition. For it embarks great wisdom and greater understanding when realized each and every day.

Repeat it at the start of each new day and discover what different nuances or new lessons that can be manifested by its expression and vocal release. You'll find that you start to look differently at circumstances and problems that were so confusing and irritating just the other day. You will find that people will seemingly recognize that you are seeking greater understanding and treat you in a completely different way. You will find an ease and comfort that you thought you had lost or had escaped you, so long ago. And you will see how much easier it could be to live in the attitudes of the great laws of Balance and Harmony, and Creator Presence. How you suddenly appreciate the simple things with less effort and how easily you can realize the true beauty of the world and the things around you.

You haven't taken a new drug or suddenly exorcised your demons; you have only revitalized your soul understandings by these simple words and the truth that we were meant to live by. These are the guidelines and confirmations that the Creator has left for us in so many places and in so many things that we've forgotten to acknowledge.

Why, because we have gotten overcome with living outside of ourselves, and lost in seeking the answers from other things and everyone else. We have strayed into believing that we must suffer and forage for the salvation we deserve. It is a given right that we have all that we need, we have all the tools to live a healthy, happy, spiritual life. Just stop to remember where it originates. Inside ourselves where the life force was placed at the beginning of our life, where the original seed of the Creator still lives in each of us.

When was the last time you asked someone how they were and they replied happy, really, really happy. I had a friend that joked that if anyone told him they were really happy he locked all the windows because he figured they were about to jump out. He wasn't kidding and neither is our modern society. It is programmed to make you think life is arduous, and tedious, and boring. Why do you think they have to remake every product that was ever invented each and every year? Because nothing is ever right. No job is ever finished. Nonsense, pure unadulterated nonsense.

Well I'm here to tell you your search is over, and the only thing left to do is, you guessed it, grow, live, and love. Stop watching the circus, it's entertaining but it just confuses our sense of what we know to be true. We have all the answers, ALL of them; we just have to remind ourselves of where we hid them.

In ascended living we must embrace all that is around us in a loving compassionate way or we will fail in our one true mission on this planet which is to seek the development and spiritual evolution of all things, not just ourselves. As a person evolves into a higher developed soul recognition they do not become more self-absorbed, they instead reach out to the universe to find a way to help others in their journey of the same, ascended living.

It is not enough to simple evolve our own soul and its understandings but we must seek out additional opportunities to shepherd others in their quest as well. We cannot force or berate them into illumination obviously, but we can extend a hand that is always available to their need for comfort and guidance. By simply accepting the responsibilities of a collective and ascended community we will have the opportunities presented to us in which to serve the greater good. And that service, or simple compassion for others, will guide our own evolution and purpose like you have never experienced before.

It is not that we have to give up our own individual life purposes and goals, it is that we reconnect with the guidance of the universal mind that better organizes ours and each others evolution. That we agree to participate in the greater good and are willing to step aside periodically in our own journey to help and guide others.

An integral part of ascended living is that we agree to always be available for the greater good no matter how seemingly divergent it may seem to our present path. That doesn't mean to sacrifice anything and everything in order to help others it just means that we make ourselves available to the opportunities that will present themselves for the advancement of our collective society. A society that in itself will then be a greater representation of all that embodies ascended living and its gifts.

It is impossible for us as individuals to be the only ones living in an ascended way as everyone around us is struggling and collapsing. It is essential to work as a whole, believe as a whole, and accept responsibility as a group ascending together. Look for the help that you can give each and every day in a small but significant amount. It will help you realize the full impact that ascended living will have on all of us when we can work as a whole and not as a separated collective.

Chapter 10

The Calamity

Staying out of the pressure cooker

The building tension we feel that is permeating every square inch of our present society is what I call the pressure cooker. Unfortunately it's not going to fully release for quite a while. Out of nowhere it seems people, events, and situations are popping up constantly in our daily lives that are almost too hard to handle. Many are too hard to even conceive of. Sure we have had our share of mindless acts throughout our recently recorded history, but today it seems that everywhere you look and read, it feels like people and things are about to become unhinged.

Out of nowhere it's like a hit and run victim is constantly being thrust before our feet, forcing us continually to side-step and weave around the mess reoccurring before us each and every day. Suddenly our idyllic lives in the 1950's, 1960's, and even 1970's is no longer available. It started in the 1980's, slowly creeping into our world and perspective. It is a selfishness and blatant disregard for our selves, each other, and the great Mother Earth.

As it accelerated into the present time, the governing bodies reacted to our own building confusion with more insane attempts to control us further. They made futile attempts to try to grasp and retain the power and mind control they thought they had over us. Making the calamity accelerate even faster. Thus building greater fears and feelings that they're trying to manipulate and regulate everything we do.

As food became more mass-produced and people started getting weaker and sicker they started to prescribe drugs to anyone and everything. From children to even animals. Crazy, just plain crazy. I remember that for most of the earlier century the last thing a doctor did was to give someone drugs when they got sick, especially a child. They felt it was the last resort knowing the importance of building ones' own immune system and how drugs counteracted that. They grew up with a bevy of natural remedies and solutions and prescribed them in most cases keeping drugs only available for extreme cases where they would use them sparingly and with caution.

With the sick getting sicker, and the masses more confused because of it, they started to manipulate the genetic make-up of the food to control not just us but the environment. Mother Nature became their next intended victim. Now that's not just crazy, but downright stupid. Ever try to stop the ocean from its force of current. Ever try to contain a bolt of lightning. Oh, but they can remake our plants better than Mother Nature had intended. Now who's confused? They are now manipulating the genetic make-up of all the food and medicines we are to consume, but with no REAL side effects we're told. Here you hold the lightning rod as the thunder storm comes in, I'm going inside to shelter where all common sense might still exist.

As the floods, pesticides, and drugs started permeating our fragile eco-system, they took no measures to correct and fix the problems. Instead they reached out and tried to control who can even grow crops. What seeds they have to use, and just how much influence we can have in the things we put in our bodies. No wonder the pressure is building, they're reacting to the building calamity as if it isn't happening. And that makes us more unbalanced and desperate for some reality, real reality not their sublimated version.

As the power schemes and manipulation begins to be more exposed. As people start to comprehend more of what the government and big businesses have been piling on us. They will attempt to try and take control of what little resources and assets we will have left. The sign of the end of the building pressure. It won't end in compromise, I guarantee that. The pressure and stakes are just too high, and have been building just too long.

So you will have to decide on whether you will concentrate on preparing yourself for self sustainability or keep watching the pressure building. Let yourself get sucked into the excuses and fake attempts at solutions, and finally be at the mercy of the dynamic outcome of the pressure cooker exploding. How long can it be plugged in before it blows its top? Time will tell. It is the systematic breakdown of our organized society in its full regalia, and it's only getting stronger.

Mother Earth can no longer ease out the pressure in a simple and noninvasive manner. She can no longer turn a blind eye to the blatant refusal of man to change his ways. His continual disregard for his own responsibility and for the negative energy he is impacting on this planet in all his selfishness and greed. You can see Mother Earth is starting to let some of the building pressure release by the clusters of earthquakes suddenly appearing in areas that haven't had earthquakes in centuries. Not only that, but hundreds of earthquakes and tremors in single a day.

As these earth changes are starting to occur, it is making people realize their need to make changes and accept new roles and ways of life, or it is fracturing people from the inside out. You can see it all around us. Unfortunately fewer people are embracing the change and showing greater compassion than those that are exhibiting the signs of starting to breakdown. Their own souls are fighting they're now patterned denial and it is making people more unstable each day. They are looking into the mirror and wondering why nothing can satisfy this now accelerating feeling of malcontent. Things that used to make them happy no longer have the desired effect. Things that they coveted in the past have suddenly lost their meaning.

It is an unsettling time if you continue to try to hang onto the past and refuse to acknowledge the need for change and a complete re-evaluation of what we think is important. What will now satisfy our soul and our desires is a completely new set of ideas. Gone are the days of financial empires and material accumulation. Gone are the availabilities for people to hoard and collect above their balanced needs. If you try to hang onto your old habits you will surely make yourself crazy in that it just doesn't have the effect it once had. We can no longer embrace a selfish, self-centered, separated society. Its vibration will not be tolerated by the planet and its own evolution helping to force our own changes.

Don't concentrate on your fleeting remembrances of what once was. Instead find the time and insight to embrace new ideas that will satisfy the soul and its true need for a balanced and harmonious life. You know you have to retake the direction of your life because we are feeling more out of control and reactionary than ever before. Take the time to find a real change and a new perspective because the harder you fight to stay the same, the more you will experience and feel the sense of everything just being wrong and incomplete. Stay out of the calamity of your unwillingness to change, and see a new beginning and its gifts.

11 chapter

Trouble in Paradise

How, When, and Why of coming Earth Changes

The earth itself is experiencing a systemic release of its own as described in the chapter on systematic breakdowns. The earth is purging the negative energies and harmful conditions that have been building up over the last few centuries. It is releasing these negative vibrations and toxic elements permeated by man and his mistaken desires and actions. Desires to control and malign himself and all of the shifting surroundings. The sun helps draw out many of these harmful elements on a daily basis. Unfortunately it has not been able to keep up with the current outpouring necessary to avert the creation of major changes now necessary to heal Mother Earth and return her to a natural balanced state.

Many major releases or regurgitation's are in their beginning stages of creation. They start their development in advance of the building tensions so that as they are needed they will rectify the buildup so that we may return to this much needed natural balance. This is not new in our long history of earth and man. Many people presently have had remembrances and experiences of these scenarios happening before. Many more have presently been getting visions and flashes of what is about to come.

A new beginning is about to unfold. Energetically, magnetically, vibrationally, physically, and spiritually. In Mother Earth, in our own physical bodies and souls, and in all the planetary bodies and elements in our current galaxy. Do not look upon these turbulent times with fear and trepidation. For many books and seers have not only prophesied this new world that is about to begin, but they have also consistently reminded us of it greatness, its newly found power, a heaven on earth they have described it. Embrace it, and all that it will have to offer.

Gone are the days of confusion, gone are the negative influences that tempt ourselves away from our true understanding and completeness. We will be left with such a brave new world that returns us to nature and our native tendencies. A drastic change from this dyslexic modern society that will not only seem in-congruent but also become incredibly impactful.

Sure you won't be able to run to the convenience store any more for your simplest needs, but the freedom and satisfaction of returning to the earth and ourselves for our daily needs will be overwhelmingly satisfying and complete. So much so that we will quickly wonder how and why we had strayed so far from this simplicity and natural way of life. You might have a glimmer of sadness for the old days of convenience but as you watch your own crops grow and saturate yourself in your own creations and ideas, you will again wonder how we had let our modern society go so far astray.

I can't comment on all the specifics of the changes as its still best to hold hope that we will embrace some illumination along the way to stem the magnitude of the earth changes that we as mankind are steering towards.

For presently we have very little awareness and acceptance of the depth of these changes as shown in our present dialogue and its lack of vision. Society as a whole continues to ignore the ever compounding catastrophes even as we speak today. Once in a 100-year floods, never before storms the size of entire countries, rainfall in hours that used to happen in over a month's time. Incredible weather patterns lining up one after another like marching armies invading a foreign land. Earthquakes, awaking volcanoes, tsunamis in mountain landscapes. All across the globe these things are happening and yet they are still trying to lead us to believe and consider them as just anomalies, crazy isolated random acts that happen to earth periodically. Well sure they have happened before in mans' and earths' recorded history, but not to this magnitude unless it is been before a great change.

As I stated before it is just starting, so it will do more good to hold positive thoughts that we as the masses will awaken quickly and in time so as not to have to endure the full wrath of complete and continued ignorance.

This happening as I call it, is not the Creators' wrath punishing us for our misdeeds and so called sins. The All in All does not realize any act as sinful or wrong, it is outside of his conception. Nor does he seek vengeance and retribution for what should be considered only our errors in thoughts and in our actions. It is the laws of the universe and our own inner conscience that is creating and executing these drastic changes.

We know instinctively that we have strayed from the goals of natural balance and truth. We have tried to ignore the laws of Compassion, Love, Growth, and Harmony. We have tried to set aside the laws of Balance and Order so that we could justify our own confused selfishness and our need to control anything and everything. We have done this in a mistaken attempt to gain and further our perceived freedom.

With such a display of contradiction it's no wonder we have to create such drastic circumstances in order to redirect ourselves on the forward path of spiritual evolution. It's not only a righting of our course, but a cleansing of our souls. The imprint created by these negative choices had embedded scars in Mother Earth and ourselves. The only way to facilitate a new beginning on earth, and a new complete way of life, is to comprehensively clean our bodies and planet of this convoluted scarring. In other words it is the only way we know how to release the imprinted negative past.

    I will give a little detail of one of the necessary earth changes and its importance. I had an incredible vision given to me one night as I was channeling this book. I want to describe it as a painting for it was beautiful in its color and definition but startling in its revelation. It depicted a landscape looking out on the horizon. Beautiful cascading mountains on the left, small trees idly grouped in a foreground cluster before the mountains. A small volcanic spout sat indiscriminately on the left in the middle of my span of sight. It was spewing gray energy that was accumulating in the sky above; its funnel of energy was forming gray ominous clouds that were overtaking the normal idyllic white clouds surrounding it. In the foreground was a man, with his body perfectly facing away from me, laying on the ground with his arms stretched out in a crucifixion-like pose, his hands open and pointing up to the sky. Upon further examination I saw, and it was mostly hidden as his positioning shielded my view, that his legs were buried or consumed up to his knees by the earth. His body was resonating and releasing a huge array of energy like the volcano but not in any color form. I was struck by the image but given no immediate understanding of the image until later that same day as I tried to recreate the vision in a pencil drawing. The earthquakes that are going to come, and nothing will stop this part of the necessary earth changes, are a complete releasing of all the negative forces that have been pummeled and encased in the earth over the last thousands of years. As man made his errors of war and bloodshed, his mistaken desires of greed and selfishness, he encased the negative expressions on the surface of the planet which in turn absorbed into the core of the planet. As this new beginning will start to unfold, Mother Earth will release all the pent-up negative forces created by man by expunging and opening up the volcanoes of the world in a random but purposeful manner.

Man simultaneously will also experience a purging and or releasing of his own embedded negative past encased in his presently configured DNA or cellular structure. We will have an evolution of the planet and our own bodies in order to expunge these negative choices. We are now embarking on their releases and are giving way to an entrance into a new world and a new body. Most importantly when these volcanoes begin to erupt, and they will take a few years to complete their release, it is the sign that we have begun the entrance into this new age. Our new beginning.

So I remind you that as we may want to react in uncertainty and concern as to what the outcome is that these changes will bring. We are not to endure any fear or pain for we have been given many signs and understandings that can be embraced that give us the knowledge and power to embark on this new beginning. Remember that these visions by oh so many that we are now entering into, have been described over and over again as a soon to be, heaven on earth.

12 chapter

Library of Congress

Obelisk, Obel-that - Keys to the Hall of Secrets

There have been many gateways built by man to gain access to all of the knowledge, secrets, and power of the universe. The pyramids are the oldest remaining examples still left standing. The Pharaohs knew that when they passed in to the next dimension they would still not be finished with their work on this world, and that they would leave their kingdom vulnerable to the next ruler and his potential failures. So in an attempt to maintain their power, and also to guide their followers still on earth with possibly more enlightenment and universal power, they built the pyramids.

Their purpose was to house their remains that would attract the return of their soul and create a gateway in which they could return to this earth. Giving them the gift and ability to still rule and protect their people.

Their followers understood that if the Pharaoh could return through the powers of the pyramid, not only would they be better protected, but the Pharaoh would return with greater knowledge from the outer dimensions and guide them in greater wisdom and insight. The pyramids created a powerful way to bridge two worlds and access the powers and knowledge of both. That's why so many were willing to sacrifice everything, even their lives to complete such a monumental task, in such a short time period of building a pyramid in a Kings' lifetime.

The plan was to entice the soul of the Pharaoh back to the main chamber of these pyramids with foods and physical items of their grand lives here on earth as before. Molded regal images of themselves in this life, attracting the pharaoh's life-force to return. Encouraging them to ignite their life-force in a new protected shell that could then be used as safe haven in their return.

The living High Priest at the time would communicate with the returned Pharaohs' soul in a re-occurring ritual in the sacred chamber getting guidance, power, and new wisdom to better the lives of his people still left behind. History records the chambers as contents of things they needed and took to the afterlife, but it was our failure in modern interpretation of its full meaning. They were not taking them with; they were placed there to entice the return of the Pharaoh to the chamber to use them in the present. They could then re-animate through the man made new shell of the sarcophagus continuing their rule.

The larger failure was that even if the Pharaoh returned a few times as hoped, the High Priest was usually not interested in really using his newly gained instructions. The High Priests quickly realized that they could use the scenario to enlarge and elevate their own personal power. Claiming they had heard the wishes of the deceased Pharaoh they then ruled by false proxy based on their own ideas and desires. That's how the High Priests became the most powerful figures in that time. They were seen as having greater insight than anyone living in that present time, being able to bridge the knowledge of two worlds. It even continued forward in most of modern history with religious figures seen to have similar powers such as cardinals, bishops, and many other prominent religious sect figures that often sat next to the kings and leaders of the time. They had as much power if not more than the designated rulers.

It is not a wrong concept, it's actually proper in its right configuration. For instance in native understandings the shamans who actually do bridge both worlds, had almost equal influence and guidance on the tribe. An incredible complement for any society in its true form but many modern civilizations lost the power of that honest insight and humility in their religious and so-called enlightened figures. They just became another individual figurehead furthering their own personal ideas and desires.

Our own Library of Congress is built in a way that symbolizes a modern gateway, much like the intended purpose of the pyramids in ancient times. It also houses all the greatest books and writings that we have accumulated in this present society. It is again similar to the Egyptians for there is actually an undiscovered library buried underground near the great sphinx which houses almost all of the writings of the greatest secrets of the universe and past civilizations. It is still undiscovered for we are not ready for all that powerful secret knowledge to be discovered yet. Our current society is not ready for such power and knowledge to be properly used.

So a complete gateway has the ability to open or bridge worlds and is also a safe house for all the accumulated knowledge collected in that civilization at that time. Quite a powerful and important building to say the least.

The Masons in power of our government at the time of its creation knew the importance and power of a gateway and built the Library of Congress to evoke similar power and to also collect accumulated knowledge for our guidance.

The gateway is really a bridge specifically for access to the akashic records. The akashic records are on a higher dimension which houses the recorded information of every event that has ever occurred in the history of the universe. Many books have been written about it, so like other subjects before, I will only summarize the pertinent parts relevant for the majority of us and our spiritual understanding.

We all have the ability to access the akashic records; we just have forgotten how to do so. The founding fathers designed the present library with symbols and architectural design that would elicit the opening of the mind to the gateway of this outer dimensional hall of records. The obelisk is a symbol of a key that can be used to open any and all records stored there. Much like a physical key used in our modern locks.

The akashic library records all the events in every lifetime of every person. But it is a neutral record. By that I mean it records no emotion, no pain, no pleasure or earthly emotions associated with these events. Furthermore it operates much like a modern computer with two different types of memory.

The forefront of readily available memory, similar to RAM in modern terms, holds the past lifetime memories that are immediately available and needed for you to progress in this present lifetime. You can consciously access them at any time.

You can also elicit them by a current lifetime living experience. They can and will without provocation spark into the forefront of our mind. Go to a place you lived before, meet someone you had a past life experience with, and it can immediately conjure up these relevant past-life memories. Remember this foreword memory bank contains only the past life memories that are needed to be remembered for our present spiritual advancement.

Pay or collect on a karmic debt, find a soul connection necessary to advance in this lifetime, or simply create the balance necessary for enlightenment by surrounding ourselves with mostly people creating similar experiences, and walking similar paths with harmonious spiritual evolution. Memories of lifetimes where we are still working with pertinent existing karma, positive or negative, presently needed to learn our current lessons.

Lifetimes where universal and earth karma have been equalized or unnecessary for this lifetimes lessons, are only available by our souls transporting to the akashic records and using a key to unlock the remembrances. The obelisk and the gateway.

The Library of Congress, the pyramids, and many other physical structures can evoke passage to the great hall of records. If you visit the pyramids or simply enter the Library of Congress you can easily gain passage to the akashic records.

But again it is a failure because we can go there without any physical gateways. Just a simple meditation and a request for access to the records in our minds-eye and we will transport there. A guide will appear to shepherd us to the outer dimension and open the gates for us. It only takes the desire of our soul and the conception of its existence for us to gain access. The key needed to unlock the additional stored lifetimes is a spiritual evolution, and an understanding to use the information only for an overview of your life and not for any earthly manipulation it could grant you in its knowledge.

13 chapter

Suspended Animation

TIME = PATIENCE

Time equals patience. *Not* if you are patient you have more time. *Not* if you could be more patient maybe it wouldn't feel that time is going so slow. Many times you try to make changes and create new things in your life and it just seems to take forever to manifest or come into your life. If you could just be a little more patient maybe it wouldn't take so long for it to finally show up.

Time *equals* patience. If there were no time you would never be impatient. Let me repeat that. If there were no time you would never be impatient. Nothing could ever be early or late. In living every moment for just that, moment by moment, there is no recognition of time. You wouldn't be aware of a past or a future and therefore you would never believe that something didn't happen on time. And isn't that an interesting statement. Happen on time. How does something happen on time? What has to happen for something to be on time? Time is a man-made construct. Something we created in order to calculate and gauge things and events that happen in our lifetime. A way to try to manipulate and control our environment. Have we lost control of our surrounding environment such that we need to fight to regain it?

The problem is now in this modern society we have to pay rent or say a mortgage every 30 days. We have to pay the water bill, the credit cards, take one pill 2 hours before the other pill, and have a check-up every 6 months, ...on and on and on.. So now we have to create money and events that will allow us to meet these time- constructed limits or we have negative ramifications. And the hamster wheel just keeps turning. So suddenly we wake up realizing that we have all agreed to a reality that says we are all living on borrowed time. And things aren't happening fast enough or are happening too fast for you and everyone who you have made these agreements with. If we simply refused to believe in this construct of time we would be the most patient person in the universe.

TIME=PATIENCE

Not having schedules of when everything has to be completed, or finished, or fixed, or paid, and we would be finally able to let the universe and ourselves return to the complete harmony and balance we were gifted with. We would never judge or be judged on how fast we did something, how long it took for us to reach a goal, acquire an understanding. Basically we would just live and return to our own inherent universal intuition of when and how we should do things.

The Mayans were one of the greatest astronomers in the history of man. In their attempt to chronicle the movement of the celestial heavens they created calendars, NOT clocks, calendars. But notice that they had calendars that centered on the movements of the moon, the sun and the stars. They even chronicled the galactic intricacies of the Milky Way and all the other planets and stars that affect each other. This helped them understand how to plant, harvest, and even fast so as to stay in near perfect harmony with all that they co-existed with. It was not an attempt to structure their lives so that they would have a means to criticize their progress. It enabled them the ability to manifest and live their lives to the fullest.

TIME=PATIENCE. Do you remember that commercial awhile back where this guy is driving his car to work and he is late? He weaves through traffic cutting people off, getting more intense as he struggles to make it ON TIME. Meanwhile another driver, seemingly oblivious to any stress or time, meanders through the same streets seeking his own separate destination. He even gets cut-off and cursed by the other incredibly impatient driver trying to force his way through traffic.

The culmination of the ad is that just as the stressed out crazed first driver arrives at his destination, rushes for the elevator to try to still NOT BE LATE, he bumps into the same guy he condemned and cut-off on the road earlier who has reached the elevator in the same building, at – you guessed it – the same TIME. They both reached their destination at the same time but experienced completely different realities. One arriving calm and in balance while the other almost having a heart attack experiencing bad traffic, uncontrollable circumstances, and basically exhausting almost all his energy before the day had even begun. To top it off he now has to ride the elevator in humiliation with the man who he had publicly cursed and condemned for moving TOO SLOW. The universe sure has a sense of humor when it can convey such powerful universal truths in such a simple TV ad.

TIME=PATIENCE. You don't have to learn how to be more patient, you have to learn how to suspend time, and or the construct of time. It has been explained by other masters as; if you can remove all expectations you will never be disappointed. But I believe that you can expect to have all that you desire, you just can't put your time limit on it. Because that dilutes all the other factors that need to occur and align themselves in order for your life to create itself in its proper grand scheme.

Many times others things, karmic debt being one of the biggest, needs to be addressed before some things can materialize and or get completed. And typically we just aren't advanced or awake enough to understand all the things that must happen before some events can take place in our lives. You want to attract the love of your love, maybe a soulmate. But you still need to make amends for how you treated that last person you loved so that you don't carry any of that negativity into this new perfect love that you so desire. You can't attract this new love until you and your old love find the circumstance necessary to forgive the past negative experiences. She's not ready to forgive you and you're not ready to acknowledge your responsibility for the collapse of the previous relationship. So you want and think you're ready for a new loving person in your life but it isn't *TIME* yet. It can get pretty myopic and overly convoluted if you constantly require a detailed explanation of why things aren't happening in your time limit. But when things seem that they aren't happening fast enough, it's because there is still work to be done on many levels before it's time for something new that your soul can undertake and accept. There is a lesson still to be learned and being impatient won't speed up time or the result you desire. Vanquish your idea of time and everything will happen ON TIME.

      Interestingly enough when you subtract time from the equation of healing you create one of the most powerful tools available. It is the greatest failure of modern medicine. The concentration and demands of man to expedite healing. A failure on mans' part to desire a quick remedy and a grand failure on the doctors who to try to deliver it. A magic pill, a quick fix, it took weeks, months, even years to create the imbalances or dis-ease and we want it all to go away in a day. A huge disconnect in the knowledge needed to be gained from illness and their lessons.

The masters say that even giving pain killers to terminal patients is a disservice to the process. I know it sounds incredibly callous and I won't go into much defense of the idea as it is an extremely entwined concept but suffice it to say that the first thing a newly diagnosed terminal patient usually does is take stock of his life. They try to figure out what they might have done to cause it. They desperately seek to find new meaning in their life, and hopefully start to immediately change their life. It brings families back together. It is a wake-up call to those around them and it is a meteor of a reminder that you need to live each day as if it were your last. If all of those gifts as they were, can erupt from just a single terminal diagnosis. If that many people can agree to change their life for the better, then there are incredibly positive benefits and gifts that can be gained from one person's seemingly tragic diagnosis.

The pain and suffering component is part of a karmic payment that is only achieved when lived through without painkillers neutralizing the experience. But the person can choose to make the karmic payment in a future life instead of the present if the pain is just too much to work through. And it doesn't mean they did anything wrong in this lifetime either.

As I stated in the earlier chapter karma is not an outside judgment. It is an internal realization of returning to balance and equalizing past negative energy and its debt. The karmic debt may be owed from a previous lifetime and have nothing to do with how the person has lived in their present lifetime. For instance a child getting cancer couldn't possibly have any reflection on the actions of their present life. But as I said I make no judgments as it is a hard pill to swallow in understanding illness. No pun intended.

In my earliest spiritual training I attended an institute that researched, experimented, and practiced many ancient and lost metaphysical practices. I was 16 at the time and the leader of the group one week explained that for the next two weeks we were going to dabble with the constructs of time. He instructed us on how to try to slow time down.

When we found ourselves rushing to an appointment, hurrying to complete a task, we were told to purposely slow down. The exact opposite of what our brain and body was telling us to do. When we felt that we just had too much to do, and not enough *time* to do it, he said we should just stop what we were doing and force ourselves to stand still for just one minute. Now when you're rushing like a banshee and you know you're late, the last thing you want to do is stand around, even for a minute. And every time the energy started to rise up inside of ourselves, and our body started to race with adrenaline, we had to stop and stand still.

Also he instructed us to have a little mantra in our head that time is slowing down thus allowing us to get everything completed in less than the amount of time we had calculated we needed. Something like; I have more than enough time to do everything that needs to be done.

It took a couple of days of concerted effort but soon I was feeling that the world was actually a little more at my control. Not only was I not stressed or rushed in doing things.

Not only did I get more done in less time. But I could actually feel time slowing down. *I was controlling time.* It was an astonishing experience at that age. I used it later in life as many successful professional athletes will attest to that time literally comes to a standstill if you really immerse yourself in the moment. A little different explanation of being in the zone as they call it but really is what happens if you break it down.

To push the envelope he instructed us to, after a couple of days, and after we think we have the hang of it, to try to schedule more things to be done in a shorter time frame. See what that does to the constructs of time. As you can maybe guess not only did I complete more than I thought possible, but it still took even less time than I had planned. Not only did time slow down and I was without stress, but strange things started to happen. A bill I was going to pay suddenly had been paid. A problem I needed to spend hours on solving suddenly solved itself, and so on. Not only had time slowed down but problems started to correct themselves and conflicts that required more time started to vanish.

I suddenly understood that our perception of time was limiting the ability for the universe to work in harmony with our own greatest good. Try it, you might like it.

In ending this chapter and in turn this book I turn to the overused adage of *time is money*. Well then if I have a lot of time then I must have a lot of money, no? Then why do people spend so much time making money. So they can then try to buy some more time later on? If we get rid of money would we then have more time? If we got rid of time would we then lose all of our money? Time and money are both man made constructs that the universe does not recognize on their own. They have to be agreed upon by more than two people otherwise they have no value and or purpose.

The Creator really did have a plan for us all; we all just forgot how simple he had made it. So let's just agree that whatever rules or man made constructs we choose to live by, we will never give up our life, our soul, and most importantly our love for one and other because we don't think we have enough time, or money, or patience.

That we all agree to live in suspended animation where there is no past and no future, just the present where love, compassion, and inner truth exist without cause or purpose. Simply living with the ultimate freewill to experience all the hidden secrets of the universe and the ability to love and be loved by all.....Konahwhaka

About the cover.........

The paper bag symbolizes our daily lunch bag prepared by our loving Mother each day for the journey from our early school years.

Each day we excitedly looked forward to the special treat she would put in our lunch bag. The surprise that was always waiting inside.

A gift to remind us of her love and attention. And that she was always looking out for us.

What would it be today we always thought. Maybe it's something new this time?

Each day you open this book may it bring the joy and excitement that our early journeys once instilled. Let it remind us that Mother Earth has a special gift just for us, each and every day we venture out into this majestic world.

Printed in Great Britain
by Amazon